Self-Love:

How to Love Yourself Unconditionally

Cylon George

ISBN: 9781521397602

Disclaimer

This book is not intended as a substitute for the medical advice of physicians. The reader should regularly consult a physician in matters relating to his/her mental health and particularly with respect to any symptoms that may require diagnosis or medical attention.

Contents

Introduction

"To keep a lamp burning, we have to keep putting oil in it."

—St. Teresa of Calcutta

Are you struggling to balance the expectations of others with your own needs and desires? In your desire to be selfless, do you consistently prioritize other people's needs over your own? Have you lost the motivation to pursue the things you once loved? Have you fallen out of love with yourself?

A good majority of us have been socialized to be suspicious of self-care. In our homes, at school, and in our houses of worship, we were taught to value service to others above all else. We the selfless are doctors and nurses, moms and dads, teachers, religious leaders, volunteers, policemen, and firefighters. We the selfless can be found in every profession and walk of life.

Though you do so much for others and the community, the good work you do may be in jeopardy if you're not keeping your own lamp filled with oil. If you're exhausted all the time, on the verge of burnout, or constantly blowing your fuse over slight annoyances, you may already know what I'm talking about but haven't been sure where to turn.

As a child, I was shy and had a severe stutter. I was regularly teased for my speech impediment, and I internalized the negative words people said about me. After enough teasing, staring, and jokes at my expense, I became sensitive.

I began to interpret every remark, look, and laugh as a personal attack. The world felt unsafe, and it was hard to be in public, especially if it meant speaking.

My emotional sensitivity remained as I grew. Even after my stuttering subsided, I was still sensitive to how others perceived me. My inner critic was born to protect my childhood self from the humiliating experiences of my condition.

I thought that if I could get people to like me, they would accept my imperfections. I thought that if I followed the expectations of others, catered to their needs, and remained silent when those needs conflicted with my own, I would be respected and thought highly of, even loved.

I thought my path to freedom from my suffering was to become totally selfless.

But my path to self-denial actually deepened my preoccupation with myself.

When it comes to self-love, we either choose the path of total self-indulgence or self-denial.

However, the spiritual teachers, sages, and mystics down the ages have shown us another path. The Buddha, after experiencing both extremes in his own life, came to enlightenment by forging a middle path. Jesus spent much of his time ministering to the poor and healing the sick. He also often withdrew from the crowds to pray and renew himself spiritually.

The journey on the middle path takes us deep inside ourselves. But this journey is not for the faint of heart. We'll navigate the emotional and spiritual minefields that cause suffering. By going directly to the source of your pain, you'll finally have the opportunity to free yourself from the beliefs and habits that keep you from loving all of who you are unconditionally.

I know. This approach is very different from others which seek to navigate you around the pain rather than through it. If you've tried these "pain free" methods before, you'll undoubtedly know that the relief is only temporary. The freedom you will find on this journey will last much longer. Instead of dreading future storms, you'll have the confidence and tools to navigate your way safely through the challenges. You'll find peace and well-being, even in the midst of storms. And by learning to love yourself well, you'll transform your life and the lives of those around you.

Chapter 1
The Case for Self-Love

"The most terrifying thing is to accept oneself completely."

– C.G. Jung

Conflicting Messages

We live in a society that has grossly distorted the idea of self-love. We struggle to truly love ourselves because we've absorbed the message that doing so means being self-indulgent or neglectful to others. We struggle to extend loving-kindness to ourselves even as we strive to extend it to others. Sometimes we even treat this type of emotional self-denial as a badge of honor.

Ironically, one of the main forces driving our collective aversion to self-love is our individualistic culture. We live in the age of selfies and "i" devices. Companies make billions by figuring out and catering to our personalized needs. We're constantly told: "Follow your dreams" or "Do what feels good to you." In media, we're confronted with images of pop stars and other celebrities who conspicuously splurge on themselves while over a billion people live on less than a dollar a day. This is what we call self-love.

Soul Love

The mixed messages we've received all our lives have created a false dichotomy within each of us. When it comes to self-care, we falsely believe that our only options are either pop culture self-love or heroic selflessness. This type of dualistic thinking has created a poverty of the soul because neither option gives us what we truly need; we've lost our ability to love and care for our very souls.

Whether we splurge on ourselves or deny ourselves, we have fundamentally lost touch with our true selves. Both attitudes are forms of escapism and denial. What are we trying to escape? Our fundamental suffering of restlessness. Catholic priest and spiritual author Ronald Rolheiser writes:

> There is within us a fundamental dis-ease, an unquenchable fire that renders us incapable, in this life, of ever coming to full peace. This desire lies at the center of our lives, in the marrow of our bones, and in the deep recesses of our soul....Spirituality is about what we do with the fire inside us.[1]

Instead of tending to the fire of our souls, we either pour gasoline on through pop culture self-love or we try to douse it with buckets of water through heroic selflessness. In our vague existential pain and suffering, we self-medicate with drugs, alcohol, work, money, status, every other conceivable addictive substance, and even by focusing on others' pain to ignore our own.

By actively trying to quench the unquenchable fire of our souls, we create much needless suffering in the world. The fire of our souls does not need quenching; instead, our souls need to love and be loved. However, our souls don't just need the love of other people—they also need our own love. To fully accept the love of others we must first love ourselves.

We do not love ourselves solely for the sake of loving ourselves: we love ourselves so we may unconditionally and completely love both ourselves and others. Our culture may be individualistic on the material level, but on the soul level we're all connected. How I treat my soul not only affects me, but also the world around me in ways I can see and in ways I cannot see. We are all intimately connected in ways we are only just barely beginning to understand.

To love the soul means to commit to tending our fires. Doing so will often be painful because it involves coming face to face with our suffering. Tending our fires involves owning up to our mistakes, facing our perceived imperfections and flaws, and getting to the root of our worries and anxieties. It means facing our chronic tendency to compare ourselves with others.

You may be forced to wrestle with the real reason why you sabotage your own happiness when everything's going well, why you end up with romantic partners who do not treat you with love and respect, or why you're stuck in menial jobs even though your education and skills could take you much further.

Tending to the fire may involve going back to your childhood to understand how the people and environment around you shaped your self-image for better or worse. Tending the fire may feel way more painful than just keeping things the way they are right now, but with acknowledgement and understanding comes self-compassion. And with compassion comes the option of letting go of the beliefs that keep you from extending love to your own soul.

The Nature of Suffering

> If there is a meaning in life at all, then there must be a meaning in suffering. Suffering is an ineradicable part of life, even as fate and death. Without suffering and death, human life cannot be complete.
>
> —Victor Frankl

Why We Suffer

Our experiences early in our lives shape who we are. Past histories likely hold important clues to why we struggle to love ourselves. Here are some common reasons:

1) You grew up in a religious tradition or household that stressed sin over grace.

If you grew up in a household that stressed human sin and depravity over grace and mercy, you will almost certainly struggle with self-love. In fact, religion is one of the primary ways we gain and perpetuate distorted images of self-love.

However, religion is not the problem itself, but rather the ways we misinterpret our faith and traditions. Within Christianity, probably the most succinct example of our misinterpretation is the way our traditions have taught us about the relationship among sin, repentance, and forgiveness.

Richard Rohr, in his book *Breathing Under Water: Spirituality and the Twelve Steps*, brilliantly summarizes how most Christians through the ages were taught to see sin and repentance:

sin > punishment > repentance > transformation[2]

In this configuration, for the wrongs of our sin to be righted, we must first experience punishment then repent in humiliating fashion before being transformed.

But Rohr argues the biblical pattern of sin and repentance is actually:

sin > unconditional love > transformation > repentance[3]

In this model, the "punishment" we receive for our sin is God's unconditional love. It's the transformation we experience in this lavishly generous encounter that finally leads to repentance, which is nothing more than resolving to turn away from the path that leads to hatred and instead taking a new path that leads to love.

2) You were parented in non-affirming ways.

If you did not grow up in a household where you were affirmed and told "I love you," you may struggle with self-love.

In some cultures, it's not customary for parents to show physical affection to their children. This is by no means an indication that they do not love their children—they are simply perpetuating the parenting styles of their own parents. Other parenting styles that inhibit your ability to fully love yourself include constant criticism, nitpicking, and overprotectiveness.

Overprotectiveness may not be an obvious contributor to our general lack of self-worth and self-love. You may think that being overprotective is how parents show love. This may be true, but it also sends a powerful signal to children that they do not have what it takes to care for themselves.

Parents, in their sincere desire to protect children from pain, either don't give children a chance to make their own mistakes and learn from them or berate them when they do.

3) You were bullied.

One of the biggest symptoms of our inability to love ourselves shows up in how we treat each other.

Almost every child knows what it's like to be bullied—unfortunately, it's become a rite of passage. But with the rise of the internet and social media, bullying has achieved new levels of intensity and cruelty. We've seen many tragic instances of young people taking their own lives because they've been publicly shamed or bullied online. Some of these attackers are so vicious and cruel that they often continue their online taunts postmortem.

Bullying is also on the rise among adults. In addition to being bullied online, adults often face bullying in the workplace by hostile coworkers and bosses. These sustained assaults on a person are hard to bear and can do tremendous damage to a person's confidence and overall sense of well-being. Often the person being bullied may feel like they are totally helpless and have nowhere to go—especially when they are bullied by a boss. Shame and fear may also drive them to remain silent and become loners.

4) You were abused or neglected.

The reality of childhood abuse and neglect is most heartbreaking. If you were abused sexually, physically, or emotionally, you're almost certain to suffer from low self-esteem.

You may harbor a deep mistrust of others and intense feelings of self-hatred. If you struggle to hold down a good job, abuse substances, or suffer from anxiety or depression, your past history may be directly connected to your present circumstances.

You may not think that there's any hope for you, but know that you are not alone. Know that you can learn to thrive through the love of others and the support of a caring and effective therapist.

5) You struggle to move on from past mistakes or regrets.

We've all made mistakes in our lives. But sometimes we're so ashamed of our past that we become stuck—often unwilling or unable to forgive ourselves and move on.

Actions that betray trust, cause physical or emotional harm, or go against deeply held values can trigger feelings of self-loathing or self-hatred.

These feelings are often accompanied by a desire to punish ourselves for what we've done, which we do in conscious and unconscious ways. Sometimes we engage in vices to numb the pain of regret. We may also unconsciously try to sabotage ourselves so that we never feel a sense of satisfaction, joy, or success.

6) You don't like certain aspects of yourself.

We all have parts of ourselves that we wish we could remove by waving a magic wand. This is especially true of our perceived character defects and physical flaws.

We glorify external beauty and tend to compare ourselves to others and judge ourselves, sometimes harshly, when we don't measure up to external standards of beauty.

People who are bullied because of their physical appearance can carry deep and painful wounds throughout their whole lives.

Self-Compassion

Most of us spend our entire lives doing everything imaginable to avoid our past suffering. Avoiding the past can cause it to haunt us. We may even unconsciously fixate on our past or use it to justify our maladaptive behaviors. However, exploring our past experiences gives us the opportunity to become aware of invisible forces that influence our behavior. This in turn gives us the opportunity to transform our self-loathing into self-compassion.

Kristin Neff, a researcher who has dedicated her career to studying self-compassion, notes that there are three specific aspects that define it:[4]

11

1. Self-kindness: Treating ourselves with kindness and understanding rather than with critical self-judgment.

2. Common humanity: The experience of being connected with others in our experiences of life rather than feeling isolated or alienated.

3. Mindfulness: The quality of being aware and present to our suffering rather than ignoring or exaggerating it.

Self-compassionate people are not immune to the suffering that comes from restlessness, self-doubt, or criticism. However, they are able to extend kindness to themselves while facing their own pain. Rather than being caught in their own ego, the self-compassionate person finds a path to healthy self-love. And by being present in their own suffering, they are able to be present to the suffering of others on a much deeper level. This is an important point because self-compassion is never just about you.

Most of us, if given a choice, will not choose to feel pain. This is understandable. No reasonable person will choose to be in pain but, according to renowned Buddhist nun Pema Chödrön, the practice of compassion "involves the willingness to feel pain."[5]

The great paradox of self-compassion is that we free ourselves from suffering not by avoiding it, but through the suffering itself.

If you can stay long enough with your own suffering, you will learn to free yourself of the suffering that causes the most pain — resentment, bitterness, unforgiving, and self-hatred. As painful as they are, these ways of suffering are all optional, and you will discover the freedom to choose your response to your circumstances and challenges.

———

12

The Interconnectedness of Soul-Love

We live in a culture that chooses separation and fear over oneness and love. Because we've lost the language of the soul, we've lost our ability to see our individuality as something utterly rooted in a larger reality beyond ourselves.

As long as we're living within our narrow notions of self, we will continue to struggle to truly love ourselves. When we conflate the self with the ego, when we constantly speak and think in terms of "I," "me," and "my," we suffer. This is the idea of self that we struggle to love because there's no room for love when we're preoccupied with ourselves.

The language of the soul points to a much deeper reality of the self that transcends the personal ego, that's connected to God and to other people, the part that continues after we die. It gives the whole self a sacred dimension.

The soul animates us and makes us who we are, yet it transcends us. The soul is powerful and immortal yet fragile and in need of our attention and love. The soul does not require perfection, yet it's made perfect when we love and accept ourselves just the way we are. Acceptance is the place where healing begins.

If you've fallen for the belief that self-love is all about you, you may resist the idea of self-love. If you've tried to become self-sufficient to numb the pain of the past, you may have only discovered the deeper pain of self-isolation. If you've become totally selfless to escape yourself, you may find yourself weighed down by exhaustion and resentment. You may have become ironically more preoccupied with yourself, not less.

To experience true inner well-being, we need to be willing to care for ourselves and others. We must see beyond the false dichotomy of having to choose between yourself and other people because loving yourself on the level of the soul simultaneously connects you with yourself and others.

Desmond Tutu and Nelson Mandela both popularized the African worldview called *ubuntu*. The meaning of the word is often translated as "a person is a person through other persons." To be fully human, we need each other. Tutu once said: "The completely self-sufficient human being is subhuman. I can be me only if you are fully. I am because we are, for we are made for togetherness, for family."[6]

Soul-love is about recognizing the interconnectedness of all aspects of our reality. It's realizing that the way we treat ourselves informs how we treat others and how others treat us. It's recognizing that some of the challenges you currently face are not of your own making. You don't have to beat yourself up for your shortcomings—just knowing you're not alone in your suffering will give you strength when you feel like giving up. It will remind you to extend the same compassion to yourself that you instinctively extend to others in their suffering.

Always remember that you can choose to respond to your necessary suffering in ways that will minimize needless suffering.

Chapter 2
Ground Zero: The Inner Critic

"There is nothing either good or bad, but thinking makes it so."

—William Shakespeare

The Voice in Your Head

Michael Singer, in his book *The Untethered Soul,*[7], talks about the "voice in your head" that's constantly narrating and judging the world around you. It never stops. Most of the time, we go about our days completely unaware of our mental dialogue—it's as effortless as breathing.

More often than not, that inner voice produces negative thoughts. It excels at amplifying our insecurities and past negative experiences. It's adept at using the past to distort our reality.

Our brains produce these thoughts so effortlessly that we almost never question them, simply taking the thoughts produced for granted. We completely identify the "self" with the "thought" because we often experience the thoughts as "I" statements:

"I'm not attractive enough, this person will never like me," or "I'm too old to pursue a new career opportunity," or "I'm not worthy of joy, love, belonging, or success."

We replay these thoughts over and over again so that they eventually become the soundtracks of our lives and cause us much needless suffering.

At the heart of this suffering is the illusion that our thoughts make up the total reality of who we are. In the words of Fr. Rohr:

> We think we are our thinking, and we even take that thinking as utterly 'true,' which removes us at least two steps from reality itself.[8]

Awareness

When confronting the voice in your head, there are varying stages of awareness you experience on the path to spiritual maturity.

The first stage is a lack of awareness of the voice. In this state, people so identify with the voice that they cannot put any emotional distance between themselves and the voice — they believe the voice without question. Unfortunately, the vast majority of people live their entire lives unaware of the voice.

The second stage occurs when people realize they are not their thoughts. They've learned to put mental, emotional, and spiritual separation between themselves and their own thoughts, not unlike the process of babies becoming self-aware individuals. Babies are born totally reliant on others and seem to be one with their mothers. They gradually develop a sense of self apart from the identity of their parents.

In the spiritual realm though, the leap between the first and second stages is gigantic and does not happen gradually, it's more akin to a waking up from a deep sleep. Waking up is not always pleasant, and waking up on a spiritual level can be just as unpleasant. Indian Jesuit priest Father Anthony De Mello writes that "spirituality means waking up."[9] Once we're spiritually awake, we can never go back to a state of total unawareness.

People reach the third state when they realize the voice is trying to help rather than harm. The self-sabotaging, incessant criticism? Really? Yes, your inner critic is actually trying to protect you, albeit in a misguided and distorted way.

In the book *Freedom from Your Inner Critic*, Dr. Jay Earley and Bonnie Weiss write:

> Your Inner Critic thinks that pushing and judging you will protect you from hurt and pain. It thinks that if it can get you to be a certain way — perfect, successful, cautious, nice, slim, outgoing, intellectual, macho, and so on — then you won't be shamed or rejected, and you might even get approval from people who are important to you.[10]

The inner critic's instinct to protect you is often based on experiences of past hurts, especially in childhood. It simultaneously attempts to protect you from past and future hurts.

Understanding the critic's positive intentions is the first step in transforming attitudes of anger and impatience with yourself into feelings of loving-kindness and compassion.

Types of Critics

There are essentially three types of inner critics:

1. The Perfectionist

The perfectionist is perhaps the most common and formidable type of critic. The perfectionist stops many people from ever attempting anything for fear that it will not be done perfectly. This often happens when your own self-worth is wrapped up with the ability to perform at the highest levels.

2. The People Pleaser

The people pleaser is also a common type of internal critic. These critics are driven by the desire to please, to be peacemakers, bridge builders, and put others at ease. You may also be extremely sensitive to the criticism of other people, which we'll address in the next chapter.

3. The Punisher

The punisher is bent on inflicting pain, perhaps due to an intense sense of inadequacy or guilt from past mistakes. A person with this critic may struggle with anger or depression. The punisher's job is to distract you from the real pain and underlying cause of your suffering.

Your Inner Critic Requires Your Participation

Though these inner critics can seem all-powerful, they are powerless without your participation. The critic can only control you if you allow it through a process that Earley and Weiss call "blending."

In blending, the various parts of the psyche at play include Self, the Seat of Consciousness, and the Critic. According Earley and Weiss, when a person is in the Self, they are connected harmoniously to other people, curious about other people in an open and accepting way, and compassionate towards others and themselves.[11] The Self they describe is similar to the concept of soul as described in Chapter 1.

The Self naturally occupies the Seat of Consciousness. Blending occurs when the critic blends with the Self, and the critic is free to take charge and negatively influence your thoughts and feelings about yourself. This process may occur unconsciously in your formative years. However, once you have wakened into awareness, you can chose whether or not to continue to participate in your inner critic's mind games.

How to Free Yourself

Once you become aware of your inner critics, you'll tend to either pretend they don't exist or try to fight them. Unfortunately, these strategies will not secure your freedom from your relentless inner critics.

Your soul does not need you to fight or flee. It needs your loving compassion, attention, and tender care. Here's a three step method to help you begin the process of unblending your soul from your inner critic:

1. Observe

To begin on your path to freedom, you must first wake up to the fact that *you are not your thoughts.*

How can you begin to embrace this idea? Simply through observation. Observe yourself as thoughts arise. Watch how you react to your own thoughts without criticizing or judging yourself or your thoughts. Simply observe.

The act of observing your own thoughts will begin the unblending process.[12] Most people learn to observe themselves through the disciplines of meditation or guided visualization. If you stick with meditating over a period of time, you'll be able to go the place of the observer quickly when you're feeling overwhelmed by your own emotions.

An immediate benefit of separating the critic from your soul is that you'll stop automatically believing everything it says to you. You'll even be able to gently question and challenge its suggestions.

2. Express Gratitude

Once your inner critic comes out of the shadows, it can be hard to feel neutral. You may feel anger or fear towards the critic, which are ok and natural. The key is to work through these feeling instead of lashing out in anger or frustration.

Recognize the fact that your inner critic was actually trying to help you all along. As misguided as its methods are for helping you, this realization will allow you to feel compassion for your critic.

Express gratitude to your critic for trying to help you the best way it knows how. This acknowledgement of the critic's efforts will allow it to relax. The critic wants to be acknowledged, heard, and even thanked for its efforts.

—

3. Face the Pain and Let Go

This is by far the hardest but most important part of the process, a step that requires you to be fully present to your suffering. You must be willing to face the very pain your inner critic worked so hard to protect you from.

You may say to yourself, "I'm not strong enough to face this pain directly." But the path to freedom runs directly through your most painful suffering.

Martha Beck, author of *Steering By Starlight*, writes:

> The raw material for joy is sorrow; the raw material for compassion is anger; the raw material for fearlessness is fear. This means that the very people who hurt you worst may turn out to have enriched you most.[13]

Whether your suffering is the result of circumstances, your own actions, or the actions of others, you have what it takes to face the pain.

How to Face the Pain

In her book, Beck describes human consciousness in three parts:

The first part she calls the shallows, where most of us spend our lives. It's primarily concerned with the material and the external, and is the part of us that harbors false fears and limiting beliefs about ourselves and others. The shallows has us "running from things [we] dread and grasping at things [we] desire."[14]

She describes the second as the core of peace, the part of the psyche undisturbed by the emotional storms of the shallows. When you're living in the core of peace, "no untruth can exist at this level of awareness: no apparent separation from the fabric of the universe, no pain, no fear, no death."[15]

The third part is the ring of fire, which serves as a barrier between the shallows and the core of peace. The only way to the core of peace is through the ring of fire. Most of us want to be in the core of peace but have no desire to go through the ring of fire. However, Beck says we must go through this emotional process to get to the core.

Going through the ring of fire is a two-part process that includes letting go of any false beliefs that cause you to suffer unnecessarily, then grieving away any unavoidable pain.[16]

In my own life, I thought that I could avoid the ring of fire caused by my speech impediment. I thought that becoming a people pleaser would do the trick. But as I matured, I realized that life did not get easier. Instead of experiencing peace, I grew even more fearful of what others thought of me. I became physically and emotionally exhausted trying to keep up with all the demands I allowed others to place upon me. I even became more resentful toward these people and myself.

Avoiding the ring of fire did not free me from pain, but rather intensified the eventual sting. I needed to finally acknowledge the set of illusions I'd allowed my inner critic to convince me were true. I needed to mourn the painful parts of my childhood; I needed to step into the ring of fire. Facing the fire meant dropping the illusions and acknowledging these truths:

- I cannot control how people perceive me, no matter how selfless I become.

- I cannot read people's minds.

- I need to speak up for myself and say no when I'm tempted to say yes.

- I need to be present in my emotional pain.

- I need to stop actively trying to hide my stutter.

I had the most trouble recognizing the last truth because it was where the rubber met the road. If I could stutter freely in public and learn to stay in the pain of my own perceptions, I would truly be walking through the fire. And that's exactly what I did.

I promised myself that I would never allow my stuttering to silence me. When I had a question in class, I spoke up. When the phone rang, I answered the call. I sought out opportunities to speak in front of groups of people. In doing so, I risked even more ridicule. Yet, instead of being mocked to death, I felt more empowered.

Instead of internalizing looks, I began to internalize this powerful quote from Eleanor Roosevelt: "No one can make you feel inferior without your consent." Because in the end, the only opinion of me that truly matters is my own.

Rather than being burned alive, the ring of fire exposed the lies and illusions that dictated my life for so many years. I began to love myself at the level of the soul, allowing me to reach the core of peace.

Is it all happily ever after? Not quite. I still sometimes struggle with my self-image, and even though I speak much more smoothly now, I still stutter. But having felt the core of peace, I'm committed to treating myself with kindness even in those moments of hurt—and those moments become fewer and fewer with each passing year.

Are you willing enter your own ring of fire? Observe, thank, and let go of your inner critic. Embrace all of who you are with deep kindness, understanding, and love. Then you'll be well on your way to your own inner transformation.

Chapter 3
Dealing with External Critics

"A critic is someone who never actually goes to the battle, yet who afterwards comes out shooting the wounded."

— Tyne Daly

In the last chapter, we confronted the biggest critic in your life: you.

We've taken a giant step forward on the path to greater self-love and self-compassion. But you're probably wondering about all the external critics in your life. We'll tackle that problem here.

We've learned that our inner critics are often trying to save us from external critics. The critic tries to protect the innocent child within us from the critics of our youth, while at the same time guarding against the pain of present and future critics. It seems to be a good plan until we realize that the criticism of others still hurts, even when we criticize ourselves first. Beating ourselves up will not help us feel better, it will just make things worse.

Once you learn how to deal with your internal critic, handling the external critics will become more manageable. In this chapter, I'll teach you some valuable tips to help you face criticism well and even use it to your advantage.

Criticism and Rejection

We tend to fantasize about a life where we never have to deal with difficult people. If our selflessness is primarily driven by a need for approval, it can painful to discover that even the most selfless people who ever lived were criticized.

No matter how kind, loving, or selfless you are someone will find fault with you while others will openly criticize and reject you.

Criticism and rejection can be very painful — there's even research to suggest that rejection activates the same region in the brain that's responsible for processing physical pain. Think about the language we use when we're rejected: "He stabbed me in the back," or "She ripped my heart out," or "That comment felt like a punch in the gut." External criticism can reinforce the negative self-critical thoughts in our heads.

When you learn to love and accept all of who you are, you'll learn to let go of the idea that you can be all things to all people. You'll accept that some people will reject you not on the basis of what you've done but because of who you are. At the level of the core of peace, your soul will be undisturbed by this fact.

How to Deal with Criticism and Rejection

The key to dealing with criticism is not avoidance, but rather learning how to manage the pain well and use it to your advantage.

Here are three steps to help you do just that and be more compassionate with yourself:

1. Maintain perspective.

Criticism is often painful because it can feel threatening. When we're being criticized, our fight or flight response gets triggered. However, criticism itself cannot harm you — only your perception of the criticism can.

So how you *choose* to perceive the criticism determines how much pain you'll feel and how long it will last.

In chapter 2, we talked about practical steps you can take to put some distance between you and your own negative thoughts. To recap they were: Observe, thank or acknowledge, and let go. You can use these same steps to put distance between yourself and the criticism of others, which will keep you from internalizing the beliefs of your critics and help you maintain a healthy perspective.

Remember, criticism will not kill you no matter how painful it feels in the moment.

2. Keep the useful while discarding the rest.

If you've been criticized a few times, you've probably figured out that not all criticism is the same (though this is easy to forget when it's happening). Another good way to manage pain is by learning to differentiate the useful from the not-so-useful. How can you know the difference?

Useful Criticism:

- Is grounded in truth.

- Is offered with compassion and kindness.

- Is affirming of what's working while offering suggestions or solutions for what's not working.

Even when criticism is useful, it can be hard to accept because it means accepting our flaws. But we all have flaws. We all have our blind spots and we all make mistakes. You don't need to be perfect. You just need to be kind to yourself and be willing to incorporate good feedback into your life.

Not Useful Criticism:

- Is only meant to be hurtful or antagonizing.

- Comes from people who never "walk their talk."

Train yourself to discard the advice of these people without giving it a second thought. Indeed, this can be hard because often these people are our own friends and family. They are major confidence killers because we've somehow learned that we're obligated to take their useless advice or toxic criticism.

But always remember this: You can love these people without taking their advice.

3. Expect it.

As long as you're around other people, you'll be criticized. You'll be criticized for doing too much, for doing nothing, for being too mean, for being too nice, for being too selfish, or for being too selfless—the list goes on. We all know it to be true, but we still fight to make reality what we want it to be. We fool ourselves into thinking that we can keep people from criticizing us, and we falsely believe that if this cannot be achieved, we'll never find peace and happiness in ourselves.

Perhaps the most important work in our lives is learning to overcome this natural instinct. We must learn to find peace even when criticized or rejected by others. If you wait for the stars to align, if you wait for everyone to approve of who you are and what you do, you'll be waiting for a long time and you'll never reach the core of peace. Your confidence, your sense of well-being, and your happiness and health cannot wait.

In order to be good practitioners of soulful self-love, we must expect criticism, even welcome it.

Chapter 4
How to Set Appropriate Boundaries

"No" is a complete sentence.

— Anne Lamott

The Importance of Boundaries

People who struggle with the idea of self-love also often struggle with setting appropriate boundaries. The concept can seem selfish, even egotistical. We often don't have a clear idea of the concept while simultaneously harboring some common misconceptions about what having boundaries actually means.

Dr. Henry Cloud, author of *Boundaries*, defines the concept this way:

> Boundaries define us. They define *what is me* and *what is not me*. A boundary shows me where I end and someone else begins, leading me to a sense of ownership.[17]

This definition demonstrates that boundary setting is not about being selfish, rude, or cruel to others. Rather it's about establishing ownership of your own thoughts, feelings, and emotions while recognizing the thoughts and feeling of others *as theirs*. When spiritual ownership gets confused, much unnecessary suffering can occur.

Few of us would question the importance of physical boundaries because they establish ownership of physical property that allows our society to function relatively smoothly and peacefully. The implications of setting spiritual boundaries are just as important, maybe even more so.

We're not taught to understand the proper place of boundaries in our lives. And good role models are hard to find. So we ignore them or worse, we're totally unaware of how our poor boundary setting skills negatively affect our well-being. Often, our boundaries tend to be either too porous or too rigid. In either case, we suffer. Do you currently have any of these symptoms?

- You feel exhausted physically, emotionally, and spiritually because you say "yes" to every request that comes your way.

- You feel resentful and bitter toward those who make excessive demands on your time and attention but lack the courage to confront your own feelings or let the other person know.

- You engage in passive aggressive behavior.

- You self-isolate.

- You're afraid of disappointing other people.

- You allow people to take advantage of you physically, emotionally, spiritually, or even sexually.

- You struggle to make your needs known to others.

- You share intimate details of your life with people you barely know.

• You feel responsible for the emotions and problems of other people and take them on as your own.

If any of these describe you, this chapter will help you set appropriate boundaries in your various relationships to ensure your well-being and protect the well-being of others.

Common Misconceptions about Boundaries

Here are some of the more common misconceptions about boundaries:

1. Boundaries are not needed in intimate relationships.

Every relationship needs boundaries to be healthy. No relationship, no matter how familial, is exempt—that includes relationships with spouses, lovers, children, parents, coworkers, extended family, and close friends. This misconception alone is responsible for a high degree of dysfunction in our families and intimate relationships.

It's actually rare for people to have boundary problems with total strangers or acquaintances. People often struggle with boundary issues in their most personal relationships. It makes sense: those who know us best may use that knowledge to manipulate us. It's an extremely painful reality that those who love us the most have the most power to hurt us. However, the solution is not to pretend that nothing's wrong for the sake of the relationship.

2. Boundary setting is for selfish people.

If you've had loose boundaries for a long time and attempt to put some in place, you're almost guaranteed to be called "selfish" by those with the most to lose. For these people, the idea of losing their power over you will cause them to do or say almost anything to keep you under their control.

If you're a naturally generous person, you may refrain from creating or enforcing boundaries for fear of being viewed as selfish and cold. But as you'll see later in this chapter, setting boundaries is one of the most generous things you can do for others. Boundary setting is not about being selfish; it's about protecting the spiritual property rights of yourself and others. Because it's not just about protecting yourself from others, *it's also about protecting others from your own potential toxic behaviors that may unconsciously occur when your needs are not being met.*

3. Setting boundaries mean being aggressive toward others.

If you're a sensitive person, this common myth can be an obstacle to setting proper boundaries. Boundary setting does not mean that you need to get in peoples' faces, have nasty arguments, or display acts of aggression toward others. In fact, aggression is a sign of poor boundaries.

Setting boundaries is really about modifying your own behavior to conform to the reality that you are limited in what you can do for others. It means recognizing that to effectively bring your authentic self to others, you must care for yourself—not as an afterthought, but in a primary way.

4. Setting boundaries involves saying "no" all the time.

Undoubtedly, learning to say "no" is a big part of proper boundary setting, but this is not the end all be all. Learning to say "no" is ultimately about learning to say "yes" to the things that truly matter in your relationships with yourself and others. In other words, "no's" pave the way to authentic "yes's."

It's also important to realize that not all boundaries are created equally. Boundaries have different levels of permeability depending on the nature of the relationship and the individual on the other end of the relationship. Boundaries tend to be more permeable when dealing with the people closest to you (quite different from having no boundaries at all) and less so when dealing with strangers. However, if the family member is highly manipulative then the boundary will need to be less permeable.

5. Nobody will like you for setting boundaries.

We resist tending to our boundaries to appear more likeable to others. If you're a recovering people pleaser like me, you'll be tempted to answer phone calls, emails, or texts immediately. You'll quietly bear the lion's share of the workload at school or in the workplace, and you're probably wearing many hats as a church or non-profit volunteer. Finally, you can be counted on to take on any other roles that nobody else wants to sign up for.

If you've lived this way for many years, upending the balance can seem daunting. Besides, everyone thinks you're a saint and you feel highly regarded by your peers. This may be true, but it's also likely that some of these people actually respect you less and view you as a pushover. Some will actively take advantage of your kindness because they know they can always get what they want from you. Are these relationships really worth protecting?

Defining your Values

Before you can begin the task of setting boundaries, you need to clearly define your values. Your values—your beliefs and attitudes—act like the operating system of your life. Whether you're aware of them or not, you live your life by a set of values, some of which may be disempowering, while others may have been hardwired into you by the environment you were raised in.

If you haven't taken the time to figure out the values you're living by, you're likely completely unaware of their presence within you and how they influence your life for better or worse. For instance, if you unconsciously believe that it's selfish to take time for yourself, you'll live your life according to those values. You'll allow yourself to live without proper boundaries that would protect you in the long run. You'll also find yourself running afoul of other important values related to patience, kindness, health, and generosity.

Once you become aware of your values, both the good and bad, the process of setting boundaries will help you decide which values are consistent with your core principles and which are not.

How to Set and Maintain Healthy Boundaries

Learning to set healthy boundaries boils down to two important skills that need to be developed:

Learning to be present with your emotions.

Learning to sit with uncomfortable emotions.

These steps are hard to execute because they require you to step into the ring of fire. However, if you're willing to experience discomfort now you'll develop more harmonious and peaceful relationships in the future.

Let's take a closer look at these two steps:

1. Be present with your emotions.

This is the first step to establishing your spiritual property lines. When you learn to be aware of, and present to, your emotions, you'll notice when resentment starts creeping in.

When you get a call from your boss at 11pm asking you to submit a financial report the next day, how does that make you feel? How about when a friend keeps you up on the phone until 1am as they pour out all their problems? Do you feel anxious, angry, bitter, or guilty for feeling all the above?

When you first begin to feel this way, it's a sign that you've hit a spiritual property line. Maybe you felt fine listening to a friend for an hour, but fifteen minutes into the second hour you start feeling a bit resentful. This moment represents your active listening property line.

Monitor your emotions during all activities. Over time, you'll build a map of your entire spiritual boundary—where you end and another person begins.

2. Sit with with your uncomfortable emotions and enforce boundaries.

This is where the rubber meets the road. Enforcing boundaries takes great courage because it means adhering to the second principle of being willing to sit with discomfort. Exercising your boundaries means *owning* what's yours and giving back to other people what's theirs.

You enforce your personal boundaries when you choose to let go of the expectations others place on you, their thoughts and feelings about you, and their own emotional upheavals. All those belong to them, which does not mean that you stop caring for other people or that you're not willing to aid them in their pain. But it's their pain, not yours, and there's nothing you can do to solve other peoples' problems. The conscious and unconscious ways we try to solve other peoples' personal problems is one of the great distortions of reality. We can walk with them and offer tools to help, but if they're not willing to take steps to help themselves, they'll remain stuck.

Maintaining your boundaries also protects others from you. When we're feeling bitter because someone's crossed a personal boundary, we may try to hide how we truly feel. We say things like "Sure, it's no problem" or "Don't worry about it." All the while, we're smoldering. You may get away with this a few times, but eventually cracks will begin to form in your armor. You'll start acting out against the other person, mostly unconsciously. Having boundaries protects others from your potential passive-aggressive behavior.

Some Strategies for Maintaining Personal Boundaries

1. Say no.

As mentioned before, setting boundaries is not just about "no's," but if this word is not a part of your regular vocabulary, it'll be impossible to maintain healthy boundaries. The really hard part about saying no is all the accompanying negative emotions . The inner critic will have his or her say: "How can you be so selfish or thoughtless?" or "If you don't answer that email today, she'll think you're a jerk" or "If I don't help they'll fall apart." Sometimes the people you say no to will also protest, especially if you've said yes for years.

But you must be willing to be uncomfortable. Instead of trying to relieve the pain by answering the email right away, ask yourself "Why do I feel this way?" Explore the underlying fears that drive the voice in your head. Think of a time when you had similar fears. Did they actually come true? Was it the end of the world or did you get through it? More often than not, there's no real basis for the fears that drive us to keep saying yes.

2. Ask for what you need.

To maintain proper boundaries, you need the cooperation of others. Boundary setting cannot be done successfully in isolation. As social beings, we need each other to thrive.

Think about it: maintaining proper physical boundaries would not be possible if the vast majority did not agree to the inherent value of maintaining property rights. No amount of protection would keep others from invading your property if this social contract no longer existed.

Similarly in the spiritual realm, maintaining boundaries means helping others understand that it's in their best interest to observe your boundaries. However, spiritual boundaries are invisible and sometimes people will invade your space without realizing they're trespassing. The most compassionate thing you can do for everyone in such a situation is to ask for what you need.

Many people would rather suffer righteous indignation in silence rather than simply ask for more space or more time. Don't assume that others can read your mind and simply give you what you need.

3. Make time for yourself.

Some will have you believe that making time for yourself is indulgent, especially when others depend on you; however, this is precisely why doing so is critical. Burnt out parents or guardians cannot adequately care for their children. Bosses who never takes time off may risk bankrupting the entire company because they lost their vision, energy, and motivation.

Making time for yourself allow you to take responsibility for all the things you own: your thoughts, feelings, emotions, and energy levels. One of the primary sources of dysfunction arises when people are willing to take on the burdens of others to avoid their own. You must beware of this seductive trap.

Schedule alone time early in the morning or in the evening. Go for solitary walks. Take your vacations. Spend a weekend alone in nature without any technology or devices.

4. Boundaries for ourselves.

This leads to the last point on how to maintain good boundaries. Boundaries are not all about who you keep out and who you let in, they're really about learning to manage yourself and your energy levels. Sometimes others' actions don't drain us, but our own do. Do you stay up way past your bedtime mindlessly watching TV? Do you spend so much time in front of computer screens that your eyes start to burn? Are you sitting all day, or taking brief walking breaks throughout the day? Practicing good boundary awareness for yourself means knowing when to adjust your behavior so that your own solitary actions do not cause you pain.

Boundary setting is critical to loving yourself. If you've had poor boundaries, working on setting appropriate boundaries in your relationships will produce many positive results down the road.

Chapter 5
Dealing with Toxic People

"Toxic people attach themselves like cinder blocks tied to your ankles, and then invite you for a swim in their poisoned waters."

—John Mark Green

While most of our external critics may actually mean well when they criticize us, there are some who criticize only to intimidate or manipulate others. They do not regard the feelings or need of others as important, especially when competing with their own needs and desires. If you regularly face intense criticism or bullying from someone you know, you're probably dealing with a toxic person. If you're still unsure, see if any of these statements resonate with you:

- They constantly monopolize your time and attention.

- They never ask you how you're doing or how they can help you.

- They're always caught up in some kind of life or death drama that needs your intervention.

- They bully or intimidate you when you don't conform to their will.

- They will try to convince you that you're responsible for their actions or misdeeds.

• You often feel bad about yourself around them.

• They say negative things to discourage you, especially when you're doing something that will reduce their power over you.

• They take advantage of your kind nature for their own personal gain.

• They'll criticize you intensely if you do anything for yourself that doesn't include them.

These are just some of the experiences that are common when dealing with a toxic person. Perhaps the most toxic people in your life are family, friends, or coworkers. Acknowledging this reality can be excruciatingly painful. However, learning how to deal with toxic people is critical to mitigating suffering and improving your well-being.

Most toxic people are often hurting themselves because they may not have received emotional support in their formative years. Some may be facing serious mental and physical illnesses. As the saying goes "hurt people hurt people." These toxic individuals clearly need love and support, but not at the expense of your own health and well-being. If you live with a toxic person, you may have tried to cure them by sacrificing yourself only to see your own health decline with no improvement in their own circumstances or condition.

Strategies for Dealing with Toxic People

When dealing with a toxic person, the steps outlined in the last chapter may not be enough to help you in your quest for self-care. Probably some of the best advice I've seen on how to deal with toxic people comes from Marc and Angel of Marc and Angel Hack Life. I've adapted the steps they recommend in their popular post "7 Smart Ways to Deal With Toxic People."[18]

1. Let them go.

If a toxic person is causing you undue pain, the most compassionate step you can take for yourself is to let them go. This will feel like anything but compassionate, especially if the person truly needs help. But if you're at the point where just thinking about the person turns your stomach, you've probably done all you could to help them with no positive results. And deep down you know it's time to let them go.

You can do this a number of ways depending on your comfort level and the temperament of the other person. If it's a friend or acquaintance, you can end the relationship in person or by writing a letter. Oftentimes, ending a relationship is not so formal. Relationships can be brought to a close by not returning calls, texts, or emails. Because a toxic person might still try to communicate with you even after you've formally ended the relationship, it's important not to return requests for communication. The attempts will usually dissipate over time. If the person is not letting up, stalking, or threatening you, you may need to get law enforcement involved.

If you're dealing with toxic family members, you may need to resort to letting them go using some of the ways described above. It's incredibly painful but absolutely critical for your long-term well-being.

If circumstances don't currently allow you to completely sever ties with the toxic person, the remaining steps may help.

2. Stop pretending their toxic behavior is ok.

It's amazing how much dysfunction we're often willing to tolerate out of love for someone close to us. We falsely believe, probably with the toxic person's help, that the most charitable thing to do is endure his or her behavior with love and self-sacrifice. Toxic people may even use religion and quote Bible passages to keep you trapped in their web of lies.

But your pretending that their behavior is ok will do no good for you or the other person, it may even exacerbate the situation. If you've been trying to keep your own feelings bottled up inside, understand that this is not being loving to yourself or others. You're seriously harming your own health by remaining silent.

You must speak up and let the toxic person know that his or her behavior is not ok. If the toxic person is not used to you speaking up, this may initially shock them. They'll probably persist, but don't give in. When you do speak up, don't blame them or accuse them. Use simple "I" statements when addressing your concerns, such as "I feel unsafe when you shout at me."

This will give the toxic person pause and maybe even give them an opportunity to adjust their own behavior.

3. Put your foot down.

When all else fails, it's necessary to let the person know in no uncertain terms that you will not tolerate being abused by them, which may mean taking drastic action to separate yourself from the toxicity. You may need to involve a third party or even law enforcement. It may mean quitting your job

---

or separating from your spouse. It may even mean that you stop all contact with your parents or your grown children until they are ready to modify their behavior toward you. Be willing to go for the long-haul if necessary.

Take 100% Responsibility for the Relationship

When dealing with highly toxic people, it's easy to simply blame them for your suffering. If you've resisted taking the steps above, even in the face of extreme abuse, take some time to consider how your own actions may be the driving force in your toxic relationship.

Here are some questions to reflect on:

- Are you holding on to unreasonable expectations of the other person even though you know better?

- Are you always blaming them for how you're feeling?

- Do you react negatively when a neutral party suggests you examine how your own behavior may be validating the toxic person's misbehavior?

If so, then you're not taking 100% responsibility for the relationship. When you own your responsibility, you'll be able to successfully withstand the influence of any toxic people currently in your life.

Chapter 6
On Confidence, Procrastination, and Motivation

"Action cures fear."

— David J. Schwartz

Many people who struggle with confidence, procrastination, and motivation mistakenly believe that they can become more confident by simply applying a few tricks and techniques. Sure, hacks may boost self-confidence in the short-term, but this confidence will be hard to maintain over time unless underlying issues are addressed.

If you have confidence issues, you're likely struggling with the idea of self-love. It's hard to appear confident or earn the respect of others if you don't think well of yourself or are constantly second-guessing yourself. It's hard to be confident if you fundamentally believe that you're not worthy of any kind of success or joy, and you cannot be confident or motivated if you're unwilling to explore and pursue your deepest needs and desires.

With low motivation comes procrastination which is the engine that powers the vicious cycle of low self-confidence and motivation.

If procrastination is the engine, fear is the gasoline that runs the engine. Fear keeps us from confidently pursuing what we truly want in life. The fear of failure and humiliation causes many people to bury their greatest dreams, goals, and desires because they're afraid others will think they're grandiose or self-centered.

In her book *A Return to Love*, Marianne Williamson wrote what has become one of the most inspirational quotes of all time:

> Our deepest fear is not that we are inadequate. Our deepest fear is that we are powerful beyond measure. It is our light, not our darkness that most frightens us. We ask ourselves, who am I to be brilliant, gorgeous, talented, and fabulous? Actually, who are you not to be? You are a child of God.

> Your playing small does not serve the world. There is nothing enlightened about shrinking so that other people will not feel insecure around you. We are all meant to shine, as children do. We were born to make manifest the glory of God that is within us. It is not just in some of us; it is in everyone and as we let our own light shine, we unconsciously give others permission to do the same. As we are liberated from our own fear, our presence automatically liberates others.[19]

Read this quote again slowly and allow its full implications to wash over you. This is self-love at its highest.

It's time to stop playing small. It's time to fully develop into the person you were meant to be. It doesn't matter if you're fifteen or fifty: the time to begin developing your confidence is now.

The work we did in the previous chapters on dealing with your inner and external critics will go a long way to helping you. But be warned that taming your internal critics will not be easy. They will continue to fight to protect you from the pain of failure and rejection. You'll be tempted to put things off, and you'll experience a lot of emotional turbulence and resistance—all natural parts of the process. If you're unaware of this, it's easy to fall for the procrastination trap.

Why We Procrastinate and Why It's So Effective at Diminishing Our Self-Confidence

There are two main reasons why we procrastinate:

- To avoid doing something we find unpleasant even when we know there's a long-term upside to doing it.

- To avoid criticism, rejection, or failure.

Here's a simple equation that sums up the meaning of self-confidence:

$$Mindset + Mastery = Self\text{-}Confidence$$

Mindset is all about the attitudes and beliefs that power your life. Are you intentional about cultivating positive thoughts about yourself and others? Do you work to maintain positivity even when the going gets tough? Are you able to stay fixed on your goals even in the face of criticism or rejection?

Mastery is all about continuously improving your knowledge or skills in fields you're passionate about. The path to mastery requires a commitment to continual study and practice.

To improve your mindset and achieve mastery, you must be willing to face the inner critic every single day. The inner critic will try to get you to renege on your commitments.

Procrastination is dangerous because it compromises both mindset and mastery. If you put off writing, you won't improve your ability as a writer and you won't feel confident as a writer. You'll succumb to the self-defeating belief that you're not a writer and play right into the hands of your critics (both internal and external).

The Three Flavors of Procrastination

Here are the three primary types of procrastinators. Which resonates most with you?

1. The Pleasure Seeker

This person is primarily motivated by what's pleasurable or easy in the short-term. These types often don't realize that taking the easy road now will lead to a difficult future—e.g., spending now rather than saving for retirement.

2. The Busy Body

This person is primarily motivated by guilt. Instead of doing what needs to be done, they do related but less important tasks to create the illusion of progress—e.g., checking email instead of calling a difficult client.

3. The Perfectionist

This person is primarily motivated by fear. They fear being judged or criticized if what they produce is not absolutely perfect, and they overthink their way out of acting—e.g., never asking a significant other for marriage because the timing's just not right.

Regardless of which kind of procrastinator you are, the end result is the same: diminished mindset, diminished mastery, and diminished self-confidence.

Motivation and the Power of Rituals

How can you control your procrastination? By taking action. If you're procrastinating for fear of how others might perceive you, taking action is the only way to break this spell regardless of how you're feeling.

If you're the pleasure seeker, you must take action even when it's unpleasant. If you're the busy body, you must take the right action even if you've gotten off course in the past. If you're the perfectionist, you must take action even when you feel unprepared.

However, to improve your motivation and achieve mastery, it's not enough to just do: you have to do consistently. This is where the power of rituals comes in. Want to master something? Create a tiny ritual around it.

Every ritual has three essential elements: a compelling "why," a set of actions done regularly and automatically, and a trigger.

The compelling "why" is crucial because it's where motivation comes from. The healthier your sense of self, the more powerful your motivations will be. Do you want to just be known as a selfless individual, or do you want to be a world changer? Do you want to care for a few hungry people, or do you want to eradicate hunger? Do you just want a paycheck, or do you want a career that brings you joy and makes a difference? This is the difference between a small and big "why".

Here's a personal example: I kiss my wife goodbye every day before one of us leaves the house. Why? Because I don't just want a good or ok marriage. I want to have an amazing marriage that's transformative and lasts a lifetime. Developing the kissing ritual might not seem like much, but the most powerful rituals are the ones we barely notice.

What's the trigger? When one of us leaves the house.

This ritual works for me because it's become a habit. We perform this ritual on good days, on bad days, when we feel like it, and when we don't feel like it. It doesn't matter. When the trigger comes, the ritual's performed because we've committed to the compelling why.

Want to become a writer? Commit to writing 100 words every day.

Want to improve your health? Commit to doing 5 push-ups every day when you get out of bed.

Want to improve your relationships? Commit to writing down one aspect of your partner that you're you're grateful for every day.

Create one tiny ritual around something you want to improve in your life and commit to doing it every day for a week regardless of how you're feeling in the moment. Track and measure how you're doing. Track your thoughts and feelings. Your self-confidence will likely improve enough for you to extend your experiment to a second week.

Before you know it you'll have created habits that will transform your life, which will not only benefit you but may also inspire others to take action.

Chapter 7
The Art of Forgiveness

"The weak can never forgive. Forgiveness is the attribute of the strong."

— Mahatma Gandhi

Learning to forgive yourself and others is fundamental to spiritual growth and self-care. Put another way, you must learn to forgive to feed your soul with the love it needs to survive and thrive: it's an essential aspect of all the major world religions and spiritual traditions.

We struggle to forgive others because we think that it involves giving a free pass to those who hurt us deeply, but practicing forgiveness is not about letting a person off easy. Rather forgiveness means freeing your soul from bitterness and anger.

We mistakenly believe that forgiveness can only take place either after the perpetrator acknowledges their wrongdoing or suffers some kind of "punishment". When we do wrong, we turn this punitive instinct toward ourselves.

Most of the ways we punish and sabotage ourselves happen outside our conscious minds—the ways we sabotage our success and happiness, the ways we belittle ourselves, and the ways we allow others to use and manipulate us all point to some deep-seated and unconscious holding back of forgiveness from ourselves.

This chapter will demonstrate how practicing forgiveness can help you overcome this self-punishment.

Forgiveness and Justice

We are a society that believe in the principle of justice. When someone's wronged, we almost immediately seek someone to blame, for better or for worse. Offering forgiveness to someone who hurt you seems to run counter to our need for justice.

So does forgiving another or yourself mean withholding justice? Does it mean that we ignore or pretend no harm was done? On these questions, Archbishop Desmond Tutu answered:

> Forgiveness doesn't mean pretending things aren't as they really are. Forgiveness is a recognition that there is a ghastliness that has happened. Forgiveness doesn't mean trying to paper over cracks. Forgiveness means that both the wronged and the culprits of those wrongs acknowledge that something happened.[20]

Forgiveness does not mean an absence of justice, but it is an acknowledgement that justice, especially retributive justice, can only go so far. It's a recognition that punishing the perpetrator can never fully restore what was present before the breach of trust or the act of violence. But, even if our path is permanently altered by our own or others' actions, there can still be acceptance and peace.

In his book *Forgiven and Forgiving*, Reverend William Countryman writes:

Forgiveness means, among other things, that we've recognized the ultimate impossibility of putting the past fully "right."[21]

Forgiveness also brings to the fore another kind of justice: restorative justice. While retributive justice includes cutting someone off from a community out of fear for the safety of others, restorative justice seeks to restore a good or right relationship between the offender and the community. On restorative justice, Countryman writes:

> But there is another conception of justice, one in which forgiveness has a great role to play. This vision of justice focuses not on the past but on the future — on building a just future characterized by peace, by shalom, which means not mere absence of conflict and harm but positive well-being.[22]

How to Practice Restorative Justice on Yourself

The model of restorative justice is a powerful tool for people who feel stuck in their past mistakes and regrets. It calls them out of self-loathing and into concrete actions that restore their relationships with others and themselves. The twelve steps of Alcoholics Anonymous are built firmly on the idea of restorative justice. These steps help people who are hurting and who have hurt others compassionately find their way back to wholeness by restoring right relationship with themselves and others. These two aspects can never be separated — to cause harm to yourself necessarily does harm to others and vice versa. So the restoration process must involve an attempt to reconcile with others because, in the end, self-compassion is never just about you. We can see how restorative justice unfolds through the twelve steps of AA:[23]

---

1. We admitted we were powerless over alcohol—that our lives had become unmanageable.

2. We came to believe that a Power greater than ourselves could restore us to sanity.

3. We made a decision to turn our will and our lives over to the care of God as we understood Him.

4. We made a searching and fearless moral inventory of ourselves.

5. We admitted to God, to ourselves, and to another human being the exact nature of our wrongs.

6. We were entirely ready to have God remove all these defects of character.

7. We humbly asked Him to remove our shortcomings.

8. We made a list of all persons we had harmed and became willing to make amends to them all.

9. We made direct amends to such people wherever possible, except when to do so would injure them or others.

10. We continued to take personal inventory and when we were wrong promptly admitted it.

11. We sought through prayer and meditation to improve our conscious contact with God, as we understood Him, praying only for knowledge of His will for us and the power to carry that out.

12. We, having had a spiritual awakening as the result of these Steps, tried to carry this message to alcoholics and to practice these principles in all our affairs.

This process is not just for people dealing with alcohol or substance addiction issues—you can adapt this to your own personal situation. Do you struggle to forgive yourself because you did something to rupture a relationship? Take some time to go through this inventory.

Forgiving Yourself When the Wronged Won't Accept Your Sincere Apology

When those we hurt are not willing to accept our attempts at reconciliation, we can remain stuck in a state of self-loathing for years or even decades. We continuously beat ourselves up to numb the pain. Do note that steps eight and nine of the twelve steps require only that we are willing to make amends and attempt to do so in the wisest way possible.

Step nine cautions us to refrain from approaching the other if we believe it will cause him or her further injury. The right response to this circumstance is not to beat yourself up, but to forgive yourself and lovingly let the other person go.

Forgiving Someone Who Does Not Acknowledge Wrongs

A common misconception about forgiveness is that it cannot be offered when the offender is not willing to acknowledge his or her wrongs. We withhold forgiveness as a way of punishing others, but in doing so we only hurt ourselves. As the popular saying goes "resentment is like drinking poison and expecting the other person to die." Or, as another popular saying often attributed to the Buddha goes, "holding on to anger is like grasping a hot coal with the intent of throwing it at someone else; you are the one who gets burned."

When we observe children, it's hard to miss the fact that they do not live by this logic. We see how quick they are to forgive without requiring an apology or even a need to understand why they were wronged. We wrongly think that children behave this way because of their naivety. But, in fact, children are masters in the art of forgiveness. We adults, weighed down by the baggage of resentment and hurt, struggle to get it right.

Forgiveness does not require the active participation of the other person. To forgive means to let go of our feelings of ill will toward the person who hurt us regardless of whether or not the other person accepts or acknowledges it. Yes, it's preferable if they did offer an apology because it can make the process easier, but it's not necessary.

Letting go of feelings of ill will always has the effect of relieving our own suffering. It means letting go of the hot coals before they do any further damage to you.

Chapter 8
Joy and Laughter

"The most wasted of days is one without laughter."

—Nicholas Chamfort

When was the last time you had a good, hearty laugh?

It's hard to deny that in our modern world, excessive levity is not something we aspire to. In fact, people who smile or laugh a lot may be viewed with suspicion—we may think they're insincere, mentally unstable, lacking more serious life goals, or maybe they want something.

But there are some people whose laughter and joy can cut right through our apprehensions and go straight to our hearts. They seem able to have joy within them on good days or bad days.

Even though most of us accept the sentiment that laughter is the best medicine for the soul, we forget to take our daily dose. For those for who tend toward selflessness, laughter may seem self-indulgent, especially in the face of a broken and suffering world. But laughter is just the medicine our suffering world needs.

Sister Anne Bryan Smollin in her book, *Jiggle Your Heart and Tickle Your Soul* writes: "There is nothing like a good laugh. It tickles our very souls. Laughter is an activity of the heart."[24]

The Laugh That Shook My Soul

As a child, I had a teacher whose laugh could be heard a mile away. He always greeted me with a hearty laugh and a warm, two-handed handshake. If something was particularly delightful to him, he would laugh so hard that I could almost feel my insides shake. The joy he experienced came from deep within his soul and went straight into mine. It was hard not to be joyful around him.

To this day, whenever I think about what it means to be joyful, my teacher comes to mind. I'm sure he had his good and bad days like anyone else, and I'm also sure there were some days when he didn't feel like laughing. But I cannot remember a day when he was negative toward me or anyone else. He taught me how to be joyful.

Joy on this level, the level of the soul, goes well beyond our popular notions of happiness and the selfish pursuit of physical or sensual pleasure. You can be in the middle of pain or suffering and still be joyful. You can even find your own joy by bringing joy to others.

If you've struggled to find joy, here are a few ideas to help you bring more joy and laughter into your life:

1. Don't wait for a reason to smile or laugh.

So many of us of miss out on the powerful medicine of laughter because we're waiting around for reasons to smile. Maybe you're waiting for a good joke, a raise, or a compliment from an important person. These are all good things, but you don't need any of them to begin experiencing joy: you can simply smile. Take a deep breath and smile the biggest smile you can muster. It may start off as fake but within moments you'll find reasons to smile genuinely.

2. Express gratitude.

As you find reasons to smile—clean air, good health, and loved ones—begin to develop a habit of expressing gratitude. Say out loud "I am so thankful for my good health and my family." Say it with intention and emotion. Keep a gratitude journal where you write all the things you are grateful for each day, large or small. On the days when you're feeling down, read a couple entries from your journal.

3. Laugh at yourself.

When things go wrong, as will inevitably happen from time to time, try to find the humor in the situation and learn to laugh at yourself. When things don't go your way, when your shortcomings are criticized, or when you make an honest mistake, laugh at yourself. You'll silence your critics, diffuse tense situations, and feel better.

4. Cultivate your inner comedian.

You may think you don't have a comedic bone in your body, but we all have the ability to bring humor and laughter to others. You don't have to be a world-class comedian to make people laugh; you mostly just need to be yourself. Besides, people are hungry for connection and developing your sense of humor will greatly enhance your relationships. It will also bring you deep inner joy.

When you cultivate joy and laughter, you'll cultivate your ability to care for your soul. You'll reduce your stress, improve your creativity, and attract others to you. You'll also become more resilient, bouncing back from setbacks, disappointments, and heartaches with relative ease.

Chapter 9
Achieving Well-Being

"All shall be well, and all shall be well and all manner of things shall be well."

—Julian of Norwich

When people say they desire happiness, most really want well-being. In this closing chapter, we'll reflect on what it means to have well-being. We tend to associate happiness with the fleeting emotion we experience when everything seems to be going our way. We experience happiness as a conditional emotion—i.e., if this thing that I really want happens, then I'll be happy. You may never say this out loud because it's often an unconscious script running in the background of your mind.

Well-being, on the other hand, is a more holistic experience; it encompasses happiness but ultimately transcends it. Well-being is notoriously hard to describe. One word that adequately expresses the core meaning of well-being is contentment. If you have a high sense of well-being, you know that you may not always get what you want, but you'll always have what you need to survive, or even thrive, in any circumstance.

Perhaps the words of Julian of Norwich, Christian mystic, captures the concept of well-being best: "All shall be well, and all shall be well and all manner of thing shall be well."

Learning to love yourself means being able to keep this perspective at all times. It will even help you maintain an attitude of loving-kindness toward yourself.

A Framework for Well-Being

In an episode of James Altucher's podcast,[25] he gave a brief definition of well-being that resonated with me. For him, well-being has three components: improved relationships, improved competence, and freedom. I was impressed by the way he was so clearly able to articulate what well-being meant to him.

Using Altucher's framework, I've formulated a series of questions that I believe cover the major areas in our lives that we need to consistently work on to experience long-term well-being:

1. *Improved relationships.*

This is the foundation of well-being. Without harmonious relationships, there can be no well-being. Take a moment now to reflect on all your relationships and ask yourself these questions:

Do you have a relationship with God?

Do you relate well with close family and friends?

Do you tend to your own needs?

Are you eating right, getting enough sleep, and exercising regularly?

Are you able to empathize with others?

Are you able to strike up friendly conversations with total strangers?

Do you generously give your time and talents?

Are you willing to be vulnerable with other people?

Do you bounce back easily from emotional hurts?

Do you take full responsibility for the quality of your relationships?

Do you forgive or hold grudges?

Do you laugh often?

Are you trustworthy?

Do you love yourself, fully and unconditionally?

2. Increased competence.

We often think of competence in relation to our professional lives, but it also matters greatly in our personal lives. Here are some questions to help you holistically explore competence:

Do you work to improve in your role as spouse, parent, friend, or coworker?

Are you able to find meaning in your activities, even the ones you don't enjoy so much?

Do you have clearly defined goals that you're pursuing in a disciplined way?

Are you comfortable in your own skin?

Are you confident in yourself and in your capacity to learn and grow?

Are you intentional about the values you live by?

Are you aware of your strengths and weaknesses?

Are you able to manage your emotions under stress?

Are you able to live in the present moment?

Are you committed to learning new skills and hobbies?

Are you open to healthy criticism and feedback?

Are you willing to fail?

3. *Freedom.*

Freedom here does not mean doing whatever you want, but rather realizing that you always have choices in the ways you think and act. Reflect now on these questions:

Do you frequently use the words "I have to" instead of "I choose to" or "I get to"?

Do you believe that others are responsible for how you feel?

Do you make decisions to fit in rather than doing what's right for you?

Are you willing to let go of beliefs and ways of thinking that have not served you well?

Do you routinely challenge your own thinking? Do you allow others to do so?

Do you experiment with your life?

Are you open to adventure and spontaneity?

Are you willing to laugh at yourself?

I hope this book has inspired you to make your self-care a top priority. This means being willing to confront your own pain and suffering with love and compassion toward yourself. Tending to your own well-being will fill you with abundant resources to meet the needs of a suffering world.

I hope you revisit the concepts presented in this book often. Take the list of questions from this chapter and review them periodically. Add to and subtract from it. Make your own.

When you take ownership of your well-being, you will be an unstoppable force for good in the world.

Did You Enjoy This Book?

Thank you so much for purchasing this book. If you enjoyed this book or found it useful, I'd be most grateful if you'd post a short review on Amazon. In addition to helping others discover this book, you'll also provide me valuable feedback that will help me improve future updates this book. It will also help me write future books that will best serve you.

Thanks for your support :)